⁴⁄08

F O R :

I thank God for the leader you already are,

and pray He will continue to guide you as you

strive to *Lead Like Jesus* with

all those who look to you for leadership.

F R O M :

D A T E :

THE
SERVANT
LEADER

TRANSFORMING YOUR HEART,
HEAD, HANDS, & HABITS

KEN BLANCHARD
AND PHIL HODGES

Published in Nashville, Tennessee, by Thomas Nelson Inc.

Designed by Lookout Design Group, Inc., Minneapolis, Minnesota

Project Editor: Kathy Baker

ISBN 0-8499-9659-7
ISBN 13-978-0-8499-9659-7

Printed and bound in Belgium

www.thomasnelson.com

TABLE OF CONTENTS

He who is GREATEST

among you shall be your SERVANT.

And whoever EXALTS himself

will be HUMBLED,

and he who HUMBLES himself

will be EXALTED.

—MATTHEW 23:11-12 (NKJV)

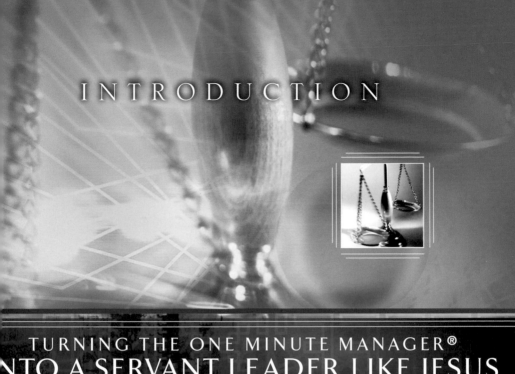

TURNING THE ONE MINUTE MANAGER®
NTO A SERVANT LEADER LIKE JESUS

Business and beliefs. Jesus and your job. Personal and professional. Servant and leader. Even seeing those words paired together makes many people uneasy. Our sophisticated culture encourages us to draw lines and keep our spiritual lives separate from our secular lives. Faith is for Sundays or family gatherings only. Right?

I, too, once modeled my life after that tired pattern, and I had a generally good, successful life. Blanchard Training and Development was alive and well. But in 1982, my world changed dramatically for the better when I encountered Jesus in a new, exciting way. At the time, I was still stunned by the runaway sales of Spencer Johnson's and my business book *The One Minute Manager*® and was looking for some sort of explanation for why our work had been so blessed.

One of the first people to point me seriously to the Lord was my longtime friend Phil Hodges, co-author of this book and the co-founder with me of the Center for *FaithWalk* Leadership. I was interested, but I didn't take the Lord into my heart completely for some time. Later, on the way to speak at a conference, I found myself sitting across the airplane aisle from successful businessman, author, and speaker Bob Buford. Talking with Bob helped me realize that we all fall short of perfection, and the only way we can close the gap between where we are and that perfection, is through a relationship with Jesus. Sensing that I was showing some interest, Bob turned me over to Bill Hybels, senior pastor of Willow Creek Community Church outside Chicago.

What a one two punch! Buford and Hybels explained grace to me in a brand new way. They opened my eyes to the power of the Word. And they taught me that as Christians, we get three consultants for the price of one—the Father who started life, the Son who lived life, and the Holy Spirit who handles the daily operations of life.

As my perspective on faith changed, so did my views on leadership change. I realized that Christians have more in *Jesus* than just a great spiritual leader; we have a *practical and effective leadership model* for all organizations, for all people, for all situations. The more I read the Bible, the more I realized that Jesus did everything I'd ever taught or written about over the years—and He did it perfectly. He is simply the greatest leadership model for all time.

What is leadership? It's an *influence process*—any time you are trying to influence the thoughts and actions of others toward goal accomplishment in either their personal or professional life you are engaging in leadership. Given that definition, you can see that Jesus is our model for leadership wherever we go—not just at work. That's why Phil and I were excited about writing this book together.

Our hope for this book.

We want you to experience Jesus in a whole different way. To grow to trust Him as the perfect One to follow as you seek to lead others. He is so clear about how He wants us to lead. He wants us to make a difference in the world we live in by being effective servant leaders.

It is our prayer and desire that this book will be the beginning of a new, exciting chapter in your personal journey to *Lead Like Jesus*. This book is designed to guide you in exploring your personal response to Jesus' call to "Follow Me" and put into action His servant leadership point of view.

So, is this a business book? Yes. Is this is self-help book? Yes. Is this an inspirational book? Yes. Simply put, it's a tool to help you to take God out of the spiritual compartment of your private spiritual life and give Him free reign in all your daily actions and relationships, especially your leadership roles.

Don't just read this book with your eyes; pull it into your heart, mind, and actions. We suggest the following steps to help you reap the greatest benefits of this book:

1. *Pray for focus and insight each time you read.*
2. *As you encounter "Aha!" ideas that challenge your leadership behaviors and motives . . . stop right there. Ask yourself how you can realign your leadership over the next two days. Be specific.*
3. *Keep a journal of your "Aha!" ideas and action steps.*
4. *Review your progress and give yourself some praise.*

We want you to trust Jesus as your leadership model, so whether you're leading in business, in nonprofit organizations, in your community, or at home, you will *Lead Like Jesus*.

Read on, and let Jesus begin the transformation in you.

— KEN BLANCHARD & PHIL HODGES

JESUS CALLED THEM TOGETHER AND SAID,
"YOU KNOW THAT THE RULERS OF THE GENTILES LORDED
OVER THEM, AND THEIR HIGH OFFICIALS EXERCISE
AUTHORITY OVER THEM. NOT SO WITH YOU.
INSTEAD, WHOEVER WANTS TO BE GREAT AMONG YOU
MUST BE YOUR SERVANT, AND WHOEVER WANTS
TO BE FIRST AMONG YOU MUST BE YOUR SLAVE—
JUST AS THE SON OF MAN DID NOT COME
TO BE SERVED BUT TO SERVE, AND TO GIVE HIS LIFE
AS A RANSOM FOR MANY."

—MATTHEW 20:25–28

Whom Do You Follow? How Will You Lead

In His instructions to His first disciples on how they were to lead, Jesus
sent a clear message to all those who would follow Him that leadership
was to be first and foremost an act of service. No Plan B was implied or
offered in His words. He placed no restrictions or limitations of time,
place or situation that would allow us to exempt ourselves from His
command. For a follower of Jesus, servant leadership isn't just an option;
it's a mandate.

The truly exciting part of following Jesus is that He never sends you
into any situation with a faulty plan or a plan to fail. Because of who
He is, when Jesus speaks on a subject He guides us in a path that is in
harmony with the molecular structure of the universe. When He speaks
on leadership, He speaks to us of what is both right and effective.

Would you hire Him? A common barrier to embracing Jesus as a role model for leadership often lies in skepticism of the relevance of His teaching to your specific leadership situations. One way of putting Jesus to the test would be to apply the same criteria to His knowledge, experience, and success that you would to the hiring of a business consultant.

Take a few moments to reflect on the following leadership challenges you might be facing and see if you would hire Jesus as your personal leadership consultant based on His earthly experience as a leader.

Does Jesus have any relevant practical knowledge or experience in dealing with the following types of leadership issues I face day to day?

(Yes/No)

_____ *Dealing with and accomplishing a mission with imperfect people*

_____ *The need to establish a clear sense of purpose and direction*

_____ *Recruitment and selection of people to carry on the work*

_____ *Training, development, and delegation issues*

_____ *Constant conflicting demands on time, energy, and resources*

_____ *Fierce competition*

_____ *Turnover, betrayal, and lack of understanding by friends and family*

_____ *Constant scrutiny and challenges of commitment and integrity*

_____ *Temptations of instant gratification, recognition, and misuse of power*

_____ *Effective handling of criticism, rejection, distractions, and opposition*

_____ *Pain and suffering in serving the greatest good*

With the answers to those questions in mind, how would Jesus do your job differently than you do? _____

_____

If you choose to accept Jesus as your leadership model and consultant, how can you get in touch with Him? _____

_____

How has He indicated His interest and willingness to help you with your daily challenges and temptations? _____

_____

The Journey. As we explore what it means to lead like Jesus we will be journeying through two internal and two external domains. The motivations of our heart and our leadership point of view can, at first, be something we can keep inside and even mask over if it suits a private purpose. Our public leadership behavior and habits as experienced by others will determine how they follow. When the Heart, Head, Hands, and Habits are aligned, extraordinary levels of loyalty, trust, and productivity will result. When they are out of alignment, frustration, mistrust, and diminished long-term productivity are the result.

Going Inside—Leadership is first a matter of the heart.

Whenever we have an opportunity or responsibility to influence the thinking and the behavior of others, the first choice we are called to make is whether to see the moment through the eyes of self-interest or for the benefit of those we are leading.

May the WORDS

of my mouth and the

MEDITATIONS of my heart

be pleasing in YOUR SIGHT,

O LORD, my ROCK

and my REDEEMER.

— PSALM 19:14

SERVANT

THE HEART

YOUR LEADERSHIP CHARACTER

Self-Serving Leaders vs. Servant Leaders.

As you consider the heart issues of leadership, a primary question you will continue to have to ask yourself is: "Am I a servant leader or a self-serving leader?" It is a question that, when answered with brutal honesty, will go to the core of your intention or motivation as a leader.

One of the quickest ways you can tell the difference between a servant leader and a self-serving leader is how they handle feedback, because one of the biggest fears that self-serving leaders have is to lose their position.

Self-serving leaders spend most of their time protecting their status. If you give them feedback, how do they usually respond? Negatively. They think your feedback means that you don't want their leadership anymore.

Servant leaders, however, look at leadership as an act of service. They embrace and welcome feedback as a source of useful information on how they can provide better service.

Another way to tell a self-serving from a servant leader is how they approach succession planning.

Self-serving leaders who are addicted to power, recognition and who are afraid of loss of position are not likely to spend any time or effort in training their replacements.

EFFECTIVE LEADERSHIP STARTS
ON THE INSIDE.
ARE YOU A SERVANT LEADER OR A
SELF-SERVING LEADER?

Devotional on Successorship

Those few words above sum up what we all would like to hear when final judgment is rendered for our efforts to make a difference. One aspect of a job well done as a servant leader is what we do to prepare others to carry on after our season of leadership is completed. Your personal succession planning efforts will speak volumes about your motives as a leader. It is likely that anyone leading from an ego involved in the promotion and protection of self is not going to spend much time training and developing their potential successor. Just as avoiding or discouraging honest feedback on a day- to-day basis is a mark of an ego-driven leader, so is failure to develop someone to take your place.

In the use of His time and efforts on earth, Jesus modeled sacrificial passion for ensuring that His followers were equipped to carry on the movement. He lived His legacy in intimate relationship with those He empowered by His words and example.

Leighton Ford in *Transforming Leadership* notes that "Long before modern managers, Jesus was busy preparing people for the future. He wasn't aiming to pick a crown prince, but to create a successor generation. When the time came for Him to leave, He did not put in place a crash program of leadership development—the curriculum had been taught for three years in a living classroom."

How are you doing in preparing others to take your place when the time comes? Do you consider them a threat or an investment in the future? Are you willing to share what you know and provide opportunities to learn and grow to those who will come after you? If not, why not? These are critical matters of the heart of a servant leader. A few minutes of brutal honesty regarding your motives as a leader are worth years of self-deception.

> *I no longer call you servants, because a servant does not know his master's business. Instead I call you friends, for everything that I learned from my Father I have made known to you.* —JOHN 15:15

Servant leaders, who consider their position as being on loan and as an act of service, look beyond their own season of leadership and prepare the next generation of leaders.

Jesus modeled the true servant leader by investing most of His time training and equipping the disciples for leadership when His earthly ministry was over.

> *I tell you the truth, anyone who has faith in me will do what I have been doing. He will do even greater things because I am going to the Father.* —JOHN 14:12-13 (NIV)

Self-Serving or Servant Leader: Which are you?

The reality is that we're all self-serving to a degree because we came into this world with self-serving hearts. Is there anything more self-serving than a baby? A baby doesn't come home from the hospital asking, "Can I help around the house?"

The journey of life is to move from a self-serving heart to a serving heart. You finally become an adult when you realize that life is about what you give, rather than what you get.

Every day leaders face hundreds of challenges to their intentions. Our adversary is waiting every day to get us to be ego-driven, to be self-serving. Every day we must recalibrate our heart. You'll never be able to say, "Now I'm a servant leader, and I'm never going to be self-serving." We're all going to be grabbed off course by our egos. Just ask yourself, "How am I going to be today? Am I going to be self-serving? Or am I going to be a servant?"

To successfully combat temptations to be self-serving we need daily to surrender our motives and actions to Christ as our guide and role model for how we should lead.

NO TEMPTATION HAS SEIZED YOU THAT IS NOT
COMMON TO MAN. AND GOD IS FAITHFUL:
HE WILL NOT LET YOU BE TEMPTED BEYOND
WHAT YOU CAN BEAR. BUT WHEN YOU
ARE TEMPTED, HE WILL ALSO PROVIDE A WAY
OUT SO THAT YOU CAN STAND UP UNDER IT.

— I CORINTHIANS 10:13

At the beginning of His ministry, we see Jesus preparing to lead by acts of submission and testing of His character.

In Matthew 3:13–17 & 4:1–11 (NKJV) we read of two key interactions.

> *Then Jesus came from Galilee to John at the Jordan to be baptized by him. ¹⁴And John tried to prevent Him, saying, "I need to be baptized by You, and are You coming to me?" ¹⁵But Jesus answered and said to him, "Permit it to be so now, for thus it is fitting for us to fulfill all righteousness." Then he allowed Him. ¹⁶When He had been baptized, Jesus came up immediately from the water; and behold, the heavens were opened to Him, and He saw the Spirit of God descending like a dove and alighting upon Him. ¹⁷And suddenly a voice came from heaven, saying, "This is My beloved Son, in whom I am well pleased."*

In His interaction with John, Jesus demonstrated two very significant attributes of servant leadership. He validated and affirmed John in his ministry and submitted Himself to the same acts of surrender to doing the right thing that He would require of others. A servant leader never asks anyone to do something they wouldn't be willing to do themselves.

> *¹Then Jesus was led up by the Spirit into the wilderness to be tempted by the devil. ²And when He had fasted forty days and forty nights, afterward He was hungry. ³Now when the tempter came to Him, he said, "If You are the Son of God, command that these stones become bread." ⁴But He answered and said, "It is written, 'Man shall not live by bread alone, but by every word that proceeds from the mouth of God.'" ⁵Then the devil took Him up into the holy city, set Him on the pinnacle of the temple, ⁶and said to Him, "If You are the Son of God, throw Yourself*

down. For it is written: 'He shall give His angels charge over you,' and, 'In their hands they shall bear you up, Lest you dash your foot against a stone.'" *7Jesus said to him, "It is written again, 'You shall not tempt the LORD your God.'" *8Again, the devil took Him up on an exceedingly high mountain, and showed Him all the kingdoms of the world and their glory. *9And he said to Him, "All these things I will give you if you will fall down and worship me." *10Then Jesus said to him, "Away with you, Satan! For it is written, 'You shall worship the LORD your God, and Him only you shall serve." Then the devil left Him, and behold, angels came and ministered to Him.*

It is easy to concentrate too much attention on the physical hardships of Jesus' fast in the wilderness experience and miss the profound spiritual conditioning for servant leadership that took place.

When tempted by three of the most universal and powerful temptations a leader can face—instant gratification, recognition and applause, and improper use and lust for power—Jesus was at His spiritual best. Notice how Jesus used the Word of God He had stored in His heart and mind to confront and defeat the devil.

As you enter into a season of leadership, the quality of your service will be a direct result of your spiritual preparation.

What's Your Leadership EGO?

In 1923, pioneer psychoanalyst Sigmund Freud defined the ego as the conscious part of a person's psyche, the part that controls thought and behavior and interprets external reality. In short, he said ego is self-awareness.

Freud's ego theory has long since fused with pop culture, and we're now used to hearing people talk about "ego trips," "bruised egos," and "egomaniacs."

But in this book, when we talk about ego, we're not talking about a psychological term; we're talking about major heart issues. At the Center for *FaithWalk* Leadership, we have two simple definitions of ego:

EGO — EDGING GOD OUT
— OR —
EGO — EXALTING GOD ONLY

It doesn't get much simpler than that.

Mastering Pride and Fear.

The temptations of life—particularly false pride and fear—make it easy for us to Edge God Out as the focus of our worship, as our source of security and self-worth, and as our primary audience and judge. When you start to Edge God Out in your daily decision making as a leader, the integrity of your leadership is quickly eroded.

When we're hypnotized by false pride, we promote ourselves by being boastful, taking too much credit, showing off, doing all the talking, and demanding attention.

When we're fearful, we are protective of ourselves at work and at home. Fearful leaders may hide behind their positions, withhold information, intimidate others, become "control freaks" and discourage honest feedback.

The results of Edging God Out in the form of pride and fear are predictable.

FEARING PEOPLE IS A DANGEROUS TRAP,
BUT TO TRUST THE LORD MEANS SAFETY.

— PROVERBS 29:25 (NLT)

Pride and fear always separate man from God, man from other people, and man from himself. Isolation is a breeding ground for EGO-clouded thinking and misdirected actions.

Pride and fear always generate unhealthy judgments about our own condition based on the successes or failures of others. Pride and fear always distort the truth into either a false sense of security or a lack of confidence and diminished self-worth.

Taking time to identify your fears and sources of false pride is a vital step to breaking their negative impact on all your relationships and your effectiveness as a leader.

When you can start to name these demons in your relationships, they lose their power over you. Phil's pastor, Byron MacDonald, said, "When I step out of a servant heart in a relationship, then I release the beast into that relationship." Tame your heart, and you tame that beast.

FOR I SAY, THROUGH THE GRACE GIVEN TO ME, TO EVERYONE
WHO IS AMONG YOU, NOT TO THINK OF HIMSELF MORE HIGHLY
THAN HE OUGHT TO THINK, BUT TO THINK SOBERLY,
AS GOD HAS DEALT TO EACH ONE A MEASURE OF FAITH.

— ROMANS 12:3

How Do We Edge God Out?

>> *When we put something else in His place as the object of our worship*
When you're making a leadership decision, what do you put in God's place as the object of your worship? Power, recognition, appreciation, money—whatever it is, it's not worth it. :: *For we who worship God in the spirit . . . put no confidence in human effort. Instead we boast about what Christ Jesus has done for us. —Philippians 3:3 (NLT)*

>> *When we rely on other sources for our security and sufficiency*
When we put our trust in something else other than the unconditional love of God, other than in His care for us, when we put our security in other things—it can be our intellect, our position, our business contacts, anything—we're counting on the temporal instead of the eternal. :: *Trust in the LORD with all your heart, And lean not on your own understanding; In all your ways acknowledge Him, And He shall direct your paths —Proverbs 3:5–6*

>> *When we put others in His place as our major audience for self-worth*
In Robert S. McGee's *The Search for Significance,* we learn that if the devil had a formula for self-worth that he would want you to buy into, it would be: *Your self-worth is equal to your performance plus the opinion of others.* If you're constantly looking to make yourself feel good or worthwhile based on your performance or the opinions of others, you're constantly going to be chasing an elusive, frustrating fantasy. :: *It is better to trust in the LORD than to put confidence in man. —Psalm 118:8*

>> *When we lose intimacy with His unconditional love, we fear intimacy with others*
One of the greatest EGO factors that self-serving leaders driven by pride and fear have is the fear of intimacy with others. Like the *Wizard of Oz* they create scary false fronts and barriers between themselves and their people rather than admit that they don't know all the answers, that they may need help. They fear if they are vulnerable with people, their leadership might be questioned. The loneliness and isolation that result from fear of intimacy leaves the leader separated from the realities of what is going on and from the good ideas that others may have to offer.

Overcoming the Demon of Pride. *"The righter you sound, the madder I get."*

Is that a familiar sentiment? That's separation by pride.

When the origin of an idea is more important than the idea itself, that's a matter of pride.

During negotiations and times of change, if you can put an idea out there for a while without its author, then you can work with it and see what happens. But if you get tied into who said it, then the idea loses its effectiveness. Pride has taken over and you have Edged God Out.

Increase your sensitivity to issues of pride. Start to be aware of the things you do as a leader in your business or in your home anytime you are more concerned about promoting yourself than serving others.

If your pride is in charge, ask yourself, "What's hurting you?" Do you really want to make a decision out of pride?

When you make decisions out of pride, know that those decisions are not going to give you the best long-term results. You might get a mile or so down the road, but such decisions won't see you through the entire trip.

Study, reflect, and act on what the Bible says about pride

PRIDE ONLY BREEDS QUARRELS, BUT WISDOM IS FOUND
IN THOSE WHO TAKE ADVICE. —PROVERBS 13:10

THE LORD DETESTS ALL THE PROUD OF HEART. BE SURE OF THIS:
THEY WILL NOT GO UNPUNISHED. —PROVERBS 16:5

PRIDE GOES BEFORE DESTRUCTION AND A HAUGHTY SPIRIT
BEFORE A FALL. —PROVERBS 16:18 (NKJV)

THUS SAYS THE LORD:
"LET NOT THE WISE MAN GLORY IN HIS WISDOM,
LET NOT THE MIGHTY MAN GLORY IN HIS MIGHT,
NOR LET THE RICH MAN GLORY IN HIS RICHES;
BUT LET HIM WHO GLORIES GLORY IN THIS,
THAT HE UNDERSTANDS AND KNOWS ME,
THAT I AM THE LORD, EXERCISING LOVINGKINDNESS,
JUDGMENT, AND RIGHTEOUSNESS IN THE EARTH. FOR IN THESE
I DELIGHT," SAYS THE LORD. —JEREMIAH 9:23—24 (NKJV)

FOR I SAY, THROUGH THE GRACE GIVEN TO ME, TO EVERYONE WHO IS
AMONG YOU, NOT TO THINK OF HIMSELF MORE HIGHLY THAN HE
OUGHT TO THINK, BUT TO THINK SOBERLY, AS GOD HAS DEALT TO
EACH ONE A MEASURE OF FAITH. —ROMANS 12:3 (NKJV)

Keep First Things First. All leaders have to confront personal pride. In fact, this ego trait—as harmful as it is to ourselves and our organizations—can become addictive. Every day we will be faced with temptations to react in prideful ways, so we will always be "in recovery."

The first step to overcoming such addiction is to get your priorities in order. The leader who does not seek the Kingdom of God first often does not seek it at all.

SEEK FIRST THE KINGDOM OF GOD AND
HIS RIGHTEOUSNESS, AND ALL THESE THINGS
SHALL BE ADDED TO YOU.

— MATTHEW 6:33 (NKJV)

Then ask yourself some hard questions:

> *Are you thinking more of yourself than you should?*

> *Who is your primary audience in life—your God, yourself, or others?*

Remember, nowhere in the Bible did Jesus promote Himself, for Himself.

Hold Lightly the Things of This World. God has

called you into a stewardship relationship for the time, talent, and
treasures He has put at your disposal for His purpose.

Richard Foster, in his book *Celebration of Discipline*, provides a
simple list of ways to cut back on distractions.

>> *Buy things for their usefulness rather than for their status.*

>> *Reject anything that is producing an addiction in you.*

>> *Develop a habit of giving things away.*

>> *Refuse to be propagandized by the custodians of modern gadgetry.
Time-saving devices almost never save time, and they must be
maintained.*

>> *Learn to enjoy things without owning them.*

>> *Develop a deeper appreciation for the creation. Get close to the
earth. Walk whenever you can. Discover once again that "the
earth is the LORD'S, and everything in it." –Psalm 24:1*

>> *Look with healthy skepticism at all "buy now, pay later" schemes.*

>> *Obey Jesus' instruction about plan, honest speech. "Simply let
your 'Yes' be 'Yes,' and your 'No,' 'No'; anything beyond this
comes from the evil one" (Matthew 5:37).*

>> *Reject anything that breeds oppression in others. In a world of
limited resources, does our lust for wealth and pleasure mean
poverty for others?*

>> *Shun anything that distracts you from seeking first the Kingdom
of God. It is so easy to lose focus in the pursuit of legitimate,
even good things. Job, position, status, family, friends, security—
these and many more can all too quickly become the center of
attention.*

Naming the Demon of Fear. *Avoiding the Trap of Toxic Fear*

We have been given the capacity to fear as part of God's design for our protection and participation with Him in a relationship of unconditional love. When the capacity to fear is directed to protecting unreliable sources of love and security, it draws us away from God and into a dangerous trap.

We're more likely to be fearful when we are heavily dependent on sources of security and measurements of self-worth that are temporary and always at risk, such as:

>> *Imperfect people and relationships*

>> *Fallible organizations and institutions*

>> *Material assets*

>> *Obsolescent skills, information, knowledge*

>> *Luck and good intentions*

>> *Past successes and future actions*

And if we're not careful, we can become addicted to using fear as an easy method of manipulation and control to produce short-term results.

Study, reflect and act on what the Bible says about Fear.

FEAR OF THE LORD

THE FEAR OF THE LORD IS THE BEGINNING
OF WISDOM. — PSALM 111:10

THE FEAR OF THE LORD IS CLEAN, ENDURING FOREVER;
THE JUDGMENTS OF THE LORD ARE TRUE AND RIGHTEOUS
ALTOGETHER. — PSALM 19:9 (NKJV)

YOU ALONE ARE TO BE FEARED. WHO CAN STAND BEFORE
YOU WHEN YOU ARE ANGRY? — PSALM 76:7

HE WHO FEARS THE LORD HAS A SECURE FORTRESS, AND FOR HIS
CHILDREN IT WILL BE A REFUGE. — PROVERBS 14:26

FEAR OF THE LORD GIVES LIFE, SECURITY,
AND PROTECTION FROM HARM. — PROVERBS 19:23 (NLT)

THROUGH LOVE AND FAITHFULNESS SIN IS ATONED FOR; THROUGH THE
FEAR OF THE LORD A MAN AVOIDS EVIL. — PROVERBS 16:6

THEN PETER BEGAN TO SPEAK: "I NOW REALIZE
HOW TRUE IT IS THAT GOD DOES NOT SHOW FAVORITISM
BUT ACCEPTS MEN FROM EVERY NATION WHO FEAR HIM
AND DO WHAT IS RIGHT." — ACTS 10:34–35

FEAR OF EXPOSURE

EVERYONE WHO DOES EVIL HATES THE LIGHT, AND WILL
NOT COME INTO THE LIGHT FOR FEAR THAT HIS DEEDS
WILL BE EXPOSED. — JOHN 3:20

MANY EVEN AMONG THE LEADERS BELIEVED IN HIM. BUT BECAUSE
OF THE PHARISEES THEY WOULD NOT CONFESS THEIR FAITH FOR FEAR
THEY WOULD BE PUT OUT OF THE SYNAGOGUE. — JOHN 12:42

FEAR OF MAN

FEARING PEOPLE IS A DANGEROUS TRAP, BUT TO TRUST THE LORD
MEANS SAFETY. — PROVERBS 29:25 (NLT)

RULERS HOLD NO TERROR FOR THOSE WHO DO RIGHT,
BUT FOR THOSE WHO DO WRONG. DO YOU WANT TO BE FREE
FROM FEAR OF THE ONE IN AUTHORITY? THEN DO WHAT IS RIGHT
AND HE WILL COMMEND YOU. — ROMANS 13:3

I, EVEN I, AM THE ONE WHO COMFORTS YOU. WHO ARE YOU
THAT YOU FEAR MORTAL MEN, THE SONS OF MEN,
WHO ARE BUT GRASS? — ISAIAH 51:12

I TELL YOU, MY FRIENDS, DO NOT BE AFRAID OF THOSE
WHO KILL THE BODY AND AFTER THAT CAN DO NO MORE.
BUT I WILL SHOW YOU WHOM YOU SHOULD FEAR: FEAR HIM WHO,
AFTER THE KILLING OF THE BODY, HAS POWER TO THROW YOU
INTO HELL. YES, I TELL YOU, FEAR HIM. — LUKE 12:5

FEAR AND THE BELIEVER

FOR GOD DID NOT GIVE US A SPIRIT OF TIMIDITY, BUT A SPIRIT OF
POWER, OF LOVE AND OF SELF—DISCIPLINE. —2 TIMOTHY 1:7

THERE IS NO FEAR IN LOVE. BUT PERFECT LOVE DRIVES OUT FEAR,
BECAUSE FEAR HAS TO DO WITH PUNISHMENT. THE ONE WHO FEARS IS
NOT MADE PERFECT IN LOVE. —1 JOHN 4:18

DO NOT BE ANXIOUS ABOUT ANYTHING, BUT IN EVERYTHING,
BY PRAYER AND PETITION, WITH THANKSGIVING,
PRESENT YOUR REQUESTS TO GOD. AND THE PEACE OF GOD,
WHICH TRANSCENDS ALL UNDERSTANDING, WILL GUARD YOUR HEARTS
AND YOUR MINDS IN CHRIST JESUS. —PHILIPPIANS 4:67

FEAR OF THE FUTURE

SO DO NOT WORRY, SAYING, "WHAT SHALL WE EAT"
OR "WHAT SHALL WE DRINK?" OR "WHAT SHALL WE WEAR?"
. . . YOUR HEAVENLY FATHER KNOWS THAT YOU NEED THEM.
BUT SEEK FIRST HIS KINGDOM AND HIS RIGHTEOUSNESS,
AND ALL THESE THINGS WILL BE GIVEN TO YOU AS WELL.
THEREFORE DO NOT WORRY ABOUT TOMORROW,
FOR TOMORROW WILL WORRY ABOUT ITSELF. EACH DAY HAS
ENOUGH TROUBLE OF ITS OWN. —MATTHEW 6:31—34

Overcoming the Demon of Fear. *Apply First Aid for Treating Toxic Fear*

With trust in the knowledge of God's care and provision for your eternal well-being in mind, here are some ways for dealing with both personal fears and fear in an organization:

> >> *Accurately assess the situation.*
>
> >> *What's at risk? What's secure?*
>
> >> *Is the danger real or imagined?*
>
> >> *What short-term action may be required?*
>
> >> *What help is available?*
>
> >> *Keep the patient—you or your organization— calm and reassured*
>
> >> *Apply trust, faith, hope and love as often as necessary*

How to Altar* My Leadership EGO.

The mirror image of Edging God Out is Exalting God Only

> Instead of Pride and Fear — Humility and confidence bring health
> to relationships and acts of leadership
>
> Instead of Separation — Community and self-acceptance result
>
> Instead of Distortion — Truth will restore and cleanse relationships

How to start Exalting God Only:

>> *Embrace an eternal perspective of the here and now in light of the then and there.*

>> *Seek to lead for a higher purpose—beyond success, beyond significance—to obedience and surrendered sacrifice.*

>> *Scrupulously assess my level of trust and surrender to what I believe about God, His Kingdom and His claim on my life and leadership.*

Follow The Twelve Steps to *FaithWalk* Leadership with others in accountability relationships over time.

1. *I admit that on more than one occasion I have allowed my ego needs and drive for earthly success to impact my role as a leader—and that my leadership has not been the servant leadership that Jesus modeled.*

2. *I've come to believe that God can transform my leadership motives, thoughts, and actions to the servant leadership that Jesus modeled.*

3. *I've made a decision to turn my leadership efforts to God and to become an apprentice of Jesus and the servant leadership He modeled.*

* This is not a spelling error, but rather a call to place your ego on the altar of obedience.

4. *I've made a searching and fearless inventory of my leadership motives, thoughts and behaviors that are inconsistent with servant leadership.*

5. *I've admitted to God, to myself, and to at least one other person the exact nature of my leadership gaps—when I behave in ways that do not make Jesus proud.*

6. *I am entirely ready to have God remove all character defects that have created gaps in my leadership.*

7. *I humbly ask God to remove my shortcomings and to strengthen me against the temptations of recognition, power, greed and fear.*

8. *I've made a list of people whom I may have harmed by my ego-driven leadership, and I am willing to make amends to them all.*

9. *I've made direct amends to such people whenever possible unless doing so would injure them or others.*

10. *I continue to take personal inventory regarding my leadership role, and when I am wrong, I promptly admit it.*

11. *By engaging in the disciplines of solitude, prayer, study of the Scriptures, and belief in God's unconditional love for me, I seek to align my servant leadership effort with what Jesus modeled, and to constantly seek ways to be a servant first and a leader second with the people I encounter in my leadership responsibilities.*

12. *Having had a "heart attack" regarding the principles of servant leadership, I have tried to carry this message to other leaders and to practice them in all my affairs.*

Be TRANSFORMED

by the RENEWING

of your MIND.

— ROMANS 12:2

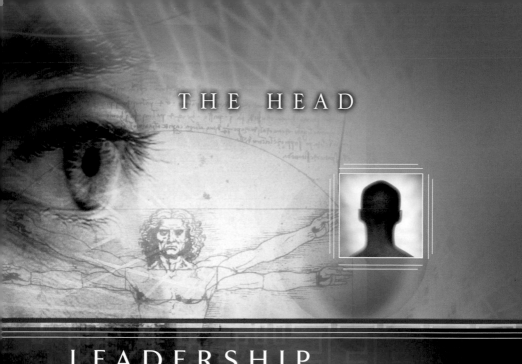

THE HEAD

LEADERSHIP
ASSUMPTIONS AND METHODS

The journey of servant leadership that starts in the Heart with motivation and intent must travel through another internal domain, that of the Head, which is the leader's belief system and perspective on the role of the leader.

All great leaders have a specific leadership point of view that defines how they see their role and their relationships to those they seek to influence. In particular, we want you to first understand the servant leadership point of view modeled and taught by Jesus, and then learn what changes in thinking are required to align your own thinking about leadership with His.

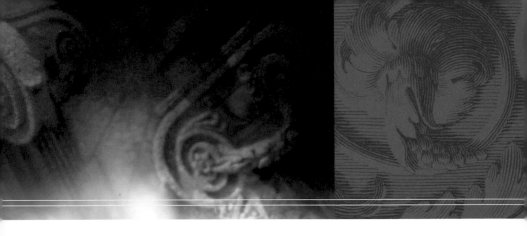

When we talk about servant leadership, most people think that means the "inmates are running the prison," or the leader is trying to please everyone. People who think this way don't understand that there are two parts of leadership that Jesus clearly exemplified:

>> *A visionary role–doing the right thing*

>> *An implementation role–doing things right*

WHERE THERE IS NO VISION,
THE PEOPLE ARE UNRESTRAINED . . .

—PROVERBS 29:18 (NASB)

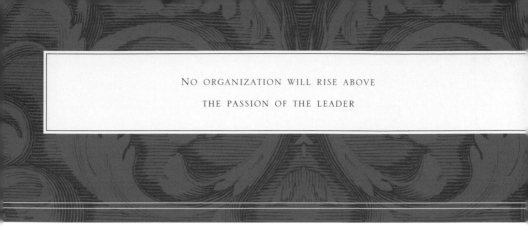

Leadership Vision. Servant leadership begins with a clear and compelling vision of the future that excites passion in the leader and commitment in those who follow. In practical terms a good vision has three parts*:

YOUR PURPOSE/MISSION: What business you are in—How will you benefit your customers?

YOUR PREFERRED PICTURE OF THE FUTURE: Where you are going—What will you look like if everything is running as planned?

YOUR VALUES: How you want people to behave when they are working on your mission and picture of the future— What do you stand for?

* Ken Blanchard and Jesse Stoner, *Full Steam Ahead: The Power of Visioning*

(Berrett–Koehler, San Francisco, 2003)

Your Purpose/Mission. *What business are you in as a person or as an organization? What are you trying to accomplish? What is your mission statement?*

Every organization should seek to improve the quality of life of its customers. Key questions to answer are:

>> *Do you know the customers you are serving as a leader?*

>> *Do you know what your customers value?*

If everyone does not understand your purpose or is not excited and passionate about it, your organization will begin to lose its way.

For instance, a congregation said they wanted to be a 24-hour-a-day church. The idea was that they had a nice facility and wanted to keep the rooms busy. But attendance was going down because the mission wasn't something people there got excited about. Your mission needs to rouse people and get them into the act of forgetfulness about themselves.

At another church, the mission is clear and uplifting. At the beginning of every service the minister says, "We believe that a close encounter with Jesus of Nazareth can transform lives. Our mission is to make Jesus smile." Backing up that statement are clear operating values and theological values. Attendance has gone up. It's a place where a community comes together with the main purpose of making Jesus smile.

A clear purpose or mission provides direction. Without clear direction your leadership doesn't matter. Even Alice learned that truth. In *Alice in Wonderland,* when she came to a fork in the road and couldn't decide which way to go, Alice asked the Cheshire Cat for advice. He asked where she was going. She said she didn't know, and the cat responded, "Then it doesn't matter which way you go."

One of the reasons organizations are bureaucratic is because no one knows what the organization is supposed to be doing. What is your purpose or mission? What business are you in that excites people?

Ken's father was a naval officer who retired early as a captain. When asked why he left the service early, he replied, "I hate to admit it, but I like the wartime Navy a lot better than the peacetime one. Not that I like to fight, but in wartime we knew why we were there and what our purpose was. We knew what we were trying to accomplish. The problem in the peacetime Navy is that since nobody knows what we are supposed to be doing, too many leaders think their full-time job is making other people feel unimportant." That's what happens when you are running an organization without a clear purpose.

When Walt Disney started his theme parks, he knew how to excite people. He said, "We are in the happiness business—we make magic!" That clear purpose drives everything the cast members (employees) do with their guests (customers).

A Preferred Picture of the Future:

YOUR IMAGE — What does a good job look like? What will the future look like if things are running as planned?

JESUS' IMAGE — Jesus outlined this for His disciples when He charged them to *"go make disciples of all nations, baptizing them in the name of the Father, Son, and Holy Spirit."* — MATTHEW 28:19

What is your preferred image of the future? Is it one that inspires you or others to share it? If someone were coming to do a documentary on your organization, whom would they talk to, what would they say, what would be happening? How would you know if you're accomplishing the vision?

Walt Disney's picture of the future was expressed in the charge he gave to every cast member: "Keep the same smile on people's faces when they leave the park as when they enter." He didn't care whether a guest was in the park two hours or ten hours. "Keep them smiling."

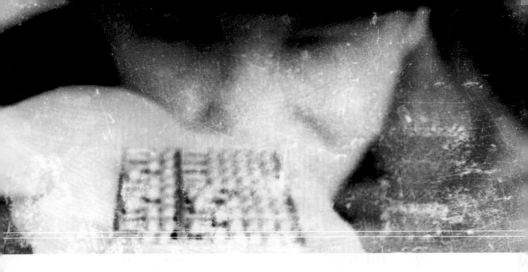

Your Values. *What do you stand for? How do you want people to behave?*

Fewer than ten percent of organizations around the world have clear, written values. But values are important because they drive people's behavior while they are working on the purpose and the picture of the future. Most organizations that do have values either have too many values and/or they are not ranked. Research shows that people can't focus on more than three or four values if you really want to impact behavior. Also, values must be ranked to be effective. Why? Because life is about value conflicts. When these conflicts arise, people need to know what value they should focus on. Walt Disney intuitively knew this when he ranked safety ahead of courtesy, the show, and efficiency among their four values. Why did he do that? Because he knew if a guest left the park on a stretcher, that guest would not have the same smile on their face as was present when entering the park. So if a cast member heard a scream while being courteous to a guest, they would excuse themselves immediately and focus on the number one value—safety.

When the Pharisees asked Jesus what the greatest commandment was,
His answer dealt with both the number of commandments and rank
order when he said:

"LOVE THE LORD YOUR GOD WITH ALL YOUR HEART
AND WITH ALL YOUR SOUL, AND WITH ALL YOUR MIND.
THIS IS THE FIRST AND GREATEST COMMANDMENT.
AND THE SECOND IS LIKE IT: LOVE YOUR NEIGHBOR
AS YOURSELF. ALL THE LAW AND THE PROPHETS
HANG ON THESE TWO COMMANDMENTS."

— MATTHEW 22:37–40

What are the key values of your organization? How are they ranked
in order of importance? True success in servant leadership depends
on how clearly values are defined, ordered, and lived by the leader.
Jesus lived His values of love of God and love of His neighbor all the
way to the cross.

NO GREATER LOVE HAS ANY MAN THAN TO
LAY DOWN HIS LIFE FOR HIS FRIENDS.

— JOHN 15:13

Acing the Final Exam. When Ken was a college professor, he was constantly in trouble with the school's faculty and was even investigated by faculty committees. The thing that drove them crazy was he always gave out the final exam questions on the first day of class. His reasoning was that not only was he going to give the exam questions to the students ahead of time, but he was going to spend the rest of the semester teaching them the answers because life is all about getting A's, not some normal distribution curve.

Bob Buford, founder of Leadership Network and author of the book *Half Time*, says he believes that all of us are going to face a "final exam" when we stand before God at the end of our lives. The two questions will be:

» *What did you do with Jesus?*

» *What did you do with the resources you were given in life?*

When you know the questions, there's no excuse not to get an A.

As a leader, let your people know what's expected so they can excel. Jesus made His expectations clear to His followers—"*I am the truth and the way. . . follow me.*"

Implementing a Clear Vision. When Jesus washed the feet of the disciples, He was transitioning His focus from the visionary/direction part of leadership to the implementation role. As He did that, He was not implying that they should go out and help people do anything they wanted. The vision was clear. He got it from the top of the hierarchy—His Father. As "fishers of men" they were to "go make disciples of all nations . . . " focusing on first loving God and then their neighbors. When it came to implementing this vision, He wanted them to be servant leaders and help people pass "the final exam."

The traditional hierarchy is good for the visionary aspect of leadership. People look to the leader for vision and direction, and although a leader should involve experienced people in shaping direction, the ultimate responsibility remains with the leader and cannot be delegated to others.

However, the implementation role—living according to the vision—is where most leaders and organizations get into trouble. The traditional hierarchy too often is kept alive and well, leaving the customers neglected at the bottom. All the energy in the organization moves up the hierarchy as workers try to please and be responsive to their bosses. The authoritarian structure too often forces the front-line people, the customer contact people, to say frustrating things like, "It's our policy," "I just work here," or "Do you want to talk to the supervisor?" In this environment, self-serving leaders assume "the sheep are there for the benefit of the shepherd." All the energy in the organization flows up the hierarchy.

Effective implementation requires turning the hierarchy upside down so the customer contact people are at the top of the organization and are able to respond to customers, while leaders serve the needs of employees, helping them to accomplish the vision and direction of the organization. That's what Jesus had in mind when He washed the feet of the disciples.

When you turn the traditional hierarchy upside down for implementation, you have the people closest to the customers—the object of your business —with all the power, all the capabilities to make decisions and to solve the problems.

For example, Ritz Carton is one of the great service organizations in this country. In the past at Ritz Carlton, every frontline associate had a $2,000 discretionary fund that they could use to solve customer problems without consulting with anybody. That's a powerful thing!

Serving the Vision. Jesus was really clear about the vision for His ministry. He was clear about the final exam.

And once a leader's vision is clear, once the final exam is set up, then a leader initiates day-to-day coaching. You prepare people to be able to pass the final exam, to live according to the vision. Leadership is not about power, it's not about control. It's about helping people live according to the vision. It's the vision—the purpose, picture of the future and values—that everyone should serve.

Jesus said, "*The Son of Man did not come to be served, but to serve*" (Matthew 20:28). And what did He come to serve? He came to serve the vision that He had been given by His Father. He came as a teacher, as a leader, as a trainer to prepare people to go out and help other

people live according to that vision. Ken followed Prison Fellowship founder Chuck Colson once during a speech when he pointed out, "All the kings and queens I have known in history sent their people out to die for them. I only know one King who decided to die for His people." That's the ultimate in service.

Jesus isn't asking us literally to die for our people. But He's saying *not so with you* (Matthew 20:26) in terms of traditional leadership. He's mandating that we set a clear vision that is going to help the world.

The vision has to be something bigger than you are. Once that's set, the Lord's mandate is servant leader behavior. Servant leadership starts with a vision and ends with a servant heart that helps people live according to that vision.

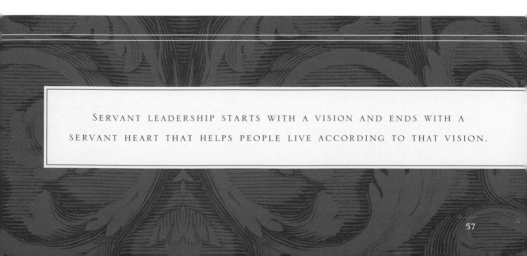

SERVANT LEADERSHIP STARTS WITH A VISION AND ENDS WITH A SERVANT HEART THAT HELPS PEOPLE LIVE ACCORDING TO THAT VISION.

Adopting a Servant Leader Point of View Will Mean . . .

STRIVING TO BE A SERVANT LEADER

You must elevate the growth and development of people from a "means" goal to an "end" goal of equal importance to the product or service mission of the organization. Servant leadership requires a level of intimacy with the needs and aspirations of the people being led that might be beyond the level of intimacy an ego-driven leader is willing to sustain.

> SERVANT LEADERSHIP STARTS WITHIN
> THE RELATIONSHIPS CLOSEST TO YOU.

UNDERSTANDING THE DIFFERENCE BETWEEN "SUCCESS" AND "EFFECTIVENESS"

"Success" can involve accomplishing short-term goals at the long-range detriment of those engaged in creating the success. "Effectiveness" accomplishes the long-range growth and development of those involved in producing the desired end as well as the result itself.

LEADING AT A HIGHER LEVEL

Effective leadership depends on whom you follow. Sustainable servant leadership behaviors will only emerge as an expression of a committed and convicted heart. As with all comprehensive theories of leadership, the doing is the hard part.

COUNTING THE COST AND PAYING THE PRICE

A servant leader in the image of Christ must be by nature a truth-teller and a realist. Honesty in communicating the price to be paid for serving and living out the values of servant leadership is a crucial test of the integrity of the leader. Jesus never minimized the cost involved in serving His vision of His kingdom. He never left people without a clear choice based on as much knowledge of both what was to be gained and what it would cost as they could comprehend

Remember that Servant Leadership Involves . . .

>> *Setting the vision*

>> *Defining and modeling the operating values, structure and behavior norms*

>> *Creating the follower environment with partners in the vision*

>> *Moving to the bottom of the hierarchy with service in mind*

"Do not merely

L I S T E N

to the W O R D ,

and so deceive yourself.

D O what it says."

— J A M E S 1 : 2 2

HANDS

LEADERSHIP BEHAVIOR

Once you know the concepts, are you really willing to change to be a better servant leader?

The journey to effective servant leadership turns outward when the heart and mind now guide the behavior of the leader in interaction with those who follow. This is where good intention and right thinking start to bear good fruit. It is where real discipleship is truly tested.

The decision-by-decision behaviors of leaders can make or break their long-range effectiveness and their ability to inspire trust. Right leadership motives and clear leadership thinking, when coupled with inept or self-serving behavior, will bring frustration and inefficiency into any leadership effort. The purpose of the Hands section of this book is to provide basic instruction in two key growth areas:

>> *Understanding the dynamics of effectively managing transformational change*

>> *Applying the concepts of Situational Leadership® II modeled by Jesus for the growth and development of people as well as accomplishing the goals of an organization*

WHATEVER YOU DO, WORK AT IT WITH ALL YOUR HEART,

AS WORKING FOR THE LORD, NOT FOR MEN,

SINCE YOU KNOW THAT YOU WILL RECEIVE

AN INHERITANCE FROM THE LORD AS A REWARD.

IT IS THE LORD YOU ARE SERVING.

— COLOSSIANS 3:23—24

NO ONE WHO PUTS HIS HANDS TO THE PLOW AND LOOKS

BACK IS FIT FOR SERVICE IN THE KINGDOM OF GOD.

— LUKE 9:62

Understanding the Dynamics of Change.

A key role servant leaders often play is facilitating necessary changes. As a result it is imperative that these leaders recognize there are four levels of change that vary in degrees of difficulty and time required.

Knowledge is the easiest and least time-consuming thing to change in people. If you want to change someone's knowledge level, send them to school, give them a book, bring in an expert on a topic, or try any other relevant means of providing information.

Attitude is emotionally charged bits of knowledge. Now people feel either positive or negative about something they know. Changing people's attitude is more difficult than changing their knowledge. Why? Because they can say, "Yes, I know . . . but I don't want to change."

Behavior is much harder and more time-consuming to change than knowledge and attitude. Why? Because now people have to do something. For instance, some people may know that smoking is bad for them (knowledge level) and they really want to stop smoking (attitude level), but the behavior is difficult to stop.

Organizational change is the most difficult change because now you are attempting to influence the knowledge, attitudes and behaviors of multiple people.

Why Is Change So Hard?

Change is a given. It will happen. Your organization will adapt or die.

As a servant leader, you have to identify which changes are necessary to implement your vision, and then help people move in that direction. Change is rarely easy, but understanding the reactions people have to change will make implementation less difficult on everyone.

react

The Seven Reactions People have to Change
—And Ways Leaders Can Ease the Transition

1. People will feel awkward, ill at ease and self-conscious when confronted by change. – *Tell people what to expect.*

2. People will feel alone even if everyone else is going through the same change. – *Structure activities that create involvement. Encourage individuals to share ideas and to work together to help each other through change.*

3. People will think first about what they have to give up. – *Don't try to sell the benefits of the change effort initially. Let people mourn their perceived losses. Listen to them.*

4. People will think they can only handle so much change at once. – *Set priorities on which changes to make, and go for the long run.*

5. People will be concerned that they don't have enough resources (time, money, skills, etc.) to implement the change.

   – *Encourage creative problem solving.*

6. People will be at different levels of readiness for any particular change. – *Don't label or pick on people. Recognize that some people are risk-takers and others take longer to feel secure. Someone who's an early adopter of one type of change might balk at another type of change.*

7. If pressure is taken off, people will revert to old behaviors.

   – *Keep people focused on maintaining the change and managing the journey.*

Valuing People and Performance.

Another key element of being a servant leader is to consider people's development as an equal end goal as their performance.

As a servant leader the way you serve the vision is by developing people so that they can work on that vision even when you're not around. The ultimate sign of an effective servant leader is what happens when you are not there. That was the power of Jesus' leadership—the leaders He trained went on to change the world when He was no longer with them in bodily form. But as He promised them and He promises us *"and surely I am with you always, to the very end of the age"* (Matthew 28:20). As we seek to leave a legacy of servant leadership behind when our own season of leadership is finished, we can do so modeling our values and investing our time in developing others.

Transformational Leadership—*Jesus as a Situational Servant Leader*

As Jesus trained and transformed His disciples from enthusiastic recruits to effective "fishers of men", He employed different leadership styles to serve their needs for direction and support. Situational Leadership® II* provides a practical framework for describing and applying the servant leadership principles that Jesus modeled.

SITUATIONAL LEADERSHIP® II:

There are three skills to being a Situational Leader: diagnosis, flexibility and partnering for performance.

SKILL #1—DIAGNOSIS

There is no single best leadership style. Leader effectiveness all depends on the development level of the person you are attempting to influence. The first skill of a situational leader is to be able to diagnose development level.

Situational Leadership® II teaches that for each task or goal people can be at different development levels based on two variables; their commitment (confidence and enthusiasm) and their competence (knowledge, skills and experience).

---

* Ken Blanchard first developed Situational Leadership® with Paul Hersey in the late 1960s. It was in the early 1980s that Blanchard and the Founding Associates of The Ken Blanchard Companies created a new generation of the theory called Situational Leadership® II. The best description of this thinking can be found in Kenneth Blanchard, Patricia Zigarmi, and Drea Zigarmi's *Leadership and the One Minute Manager* (New York: William Morrow, 1985).

Four basic combinations of commitment and competence can determine a person's development level:

ENTHUSIASTIC BEGINNERS
(Development Level 1)
People with high levels of commitment to the task but low levels of competence because they have never done this particular task before.

EXAMPLE: *A fifteen-year-old teenager the day she gets her learner's permit to drive. She is filled with excitement and confidence but knows little about driving.*

DISILLUSIONED LEARNERS
(Development Level 2)
People with some experience and competence but reduced levels of commitment and enthusiasm due to some failure during the learning process or realization that the task is harder than they thought.

EXAMPLE: *A teenager, beginning to cry after continually stalling on her first test drive.*

CAPABLE BUT CAUTIOUS PERFORMERS
(Development Level 3)

People with moderate to high levels of competence but may have lost some of their enthusiasm or confidence or are cautious in performing the task on their own.

E X A M P L E : *A teenager, getting nervous and failing her driving test, even though she had an A in Driver's Education.*

PEAK PERFORMERS/SELF-RELIANT ACHIEVERS
(Development Level 4)

People who are highly competent and highly committed to perform a particular task.

E X A M P L E : *A teenager passing her driver's test with flying colors and being permitted to drive herself to school every day.*

SKILL #2 — FLEXIBILITY

Once you know what people's development level is, you need to give them the right leadership style. You have to be flexible and able to use a variety of leadership styles comfortably to help the individuals achieve their goals or tasks.

Situational Leadership® II describes two types of leader behavior you can use in attempting to help people develop:

DIRECTIVE BEHAVIOR — *Telling people what to do, when to do it, where to do it and how to do it.*

SUPPORTIVE BEHAVIOR — *Listening to people, involving them in decision making, encouraging them, praising their progress and facilitating their interaction with others.*

Four Leadership Styles.

There are four basic combinations of directive and supportive behaviors that a leader can use:

DIRECTING (STYLE 1) — *high direction, low support*

Leaders provide specific directions about roles and goals and closely track performance in order to provide frequent feedback on results.

> EXAMPLE: *When a teenager's father tells her the exact sequence of the things she needs to do before turning on the ignition on her first test drive.*

COACHING (STYLE 2) — *high direction, high support*

Leaders explain why, solicit suggestions, praise progress that is approximately right, but continue to direct task accomplishment.

> EXAMPLE: *After a teenager stops crying during her first test drive, her father praises his daughter for excellent work on adjusting the mirror and fastening her seat belt, but then has her repeat back to him the instructions for letting out the clutch before starting the car again.*

SUPPORTING (STYLE 3) — *high support, low direction*

Leaders facilitate interaction with others, listen to people, draw them out, encourage and support them, but provide little direction.

> EXAMPLE: *A father hugging his daughter after she fails her first driving test and encouraging her to take the wheel to drive them home.*

DELEGATING (STYLE 4) — *low support, low direction*

Leaders empower their people to act independently with appropriate resources to get the job done.

> EXAMPLE: *Parents letting their teenager drive herself to school every day.*

Leaders must determine with their people how to work together in a way their people can accomplish their goals, and then they must follow through on any agreements. This involves leaders providing the right leadership for the right development level. This is exactly what Jesus did as He transformed the disciples from enthusiastic beginners to peak performers.

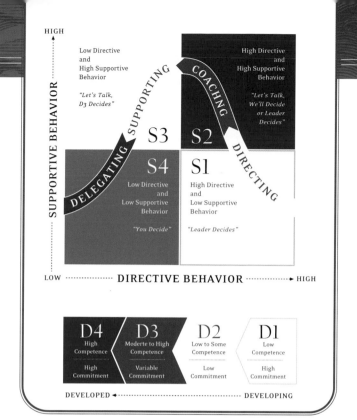

Jesus as a Situational Leader.

THE DISCIPLES AS ENTHUSIASTIC BEGINNERS (D1)
—Low Competence, High Commitment

In Matthew 4:18-22 we read:

> "As Jesus was walking beside the Sea of Galilee, He saw two brothers, Simon called Peter and his brother Andrew. They were casting a net into the lake, for they were fishermen. 'Come, follow Me,' Jesus said, 'and I will make you fishers of men.' At once they left their nets and followed Him. Going on from there, He saw two other brothers, James son of Zebedee and his brother John. They were in a boat with their father, Zebedee, preparing their nets. Jesus called them, and immediately they left the boat and their father and followed Him."

Jesus saw in these hardworking fishermen the raw material for the future leaders of the mission He would leave in their care when His season of earthly ministry was completed. In their enthusiasm, they literally dropped what they were doing when he called them to the higher purpose of being fishers of men. While they were highly committed they had little or no idea of how to accomplish their new task.

JESUS USING A DIRECTIVE LEADERSHIP STYLE (S1)
– High Directive and Low Supportive Behavior

Enthusiastic beginners (D1) need a directing leadership style (S1)— High Directive Behavior and Low Supporting Behavior

Jesus used an appropriate directing leadership style with these enthusiastic beginners when He first sent them out for the first time to act as His ambassadors (Apostles).

Jesus sent the twelve disciples out with these instructions: . . . *"Heal the sick, raise the dead, cure those with leprosy, and cast out demons. Give as freely as you have received! Don't take any money with you. Don't carry a traveler's bag with an extra coat and sandals or even a walking stick, Don't hesitate to accept hospitality, because those who work deserve to be fed."* — MATTHEW 10:5-10

THE DISCIPLES AS DISILLUSIONED LEARNERS (D2)
— *Low Competence, Low Commitment*

> *"Lord, have mercy on my son," he said. "He has seizures and is suffering greatly. He often falls into the fire or into the water. I brought him to Your disciples, but they could not heal him."* — MATTHEW 17:15-16

> (After Jesus healed the boy)
> *The disciples came to Jesus in private and asked, "Why couldn't we drive it out?* — MATTHEW 17:19

When the disciples were new to the task of being fishers of men they experienced a set back to their confidence when they discovered they were not competent to handle every situation. It is easy to imagine their disillusionment as they sought an explanation from Jesus in private. Observe how Jesus responded to their disillusionment.

Jesus Using A Coaching Style of Leadership (S2)
—High Directive, High Supportive Behavior
Disillusioned learners (D2) need a coaching leadership style (S2)—high direction, high support

Jesus used an appropriate coaching style to respond to the disciples' disillusionment when He replied to their question:

Because you have so little faith. I tell you the truth, if you have faith as small as a mustard seed, you can say to this mountain, "Move from here to there" and it will move. Nothing will be impossible for you.
—Matthew 17:20

Did you notice? Jesus did not scold the disciples. He did not lose His temper with them. Instead, He gave them the support they needed when their commitment was low, but He also gave them very specific direction on why they could not heal the boy. Nowhere in the Scriptures do we find a time when Jesus blasted the disciples because of a mistake they made. The true Situational Leader makes the necessary adjustments in leadership style to help the individual become a self-reliant achiever without losing his or her temper.

PETER AS A CAPABLE BUT CAUTIOUS PERFORMER (D3)
—*Moderate to High Competence, Variable Commitment*

> *When the disciples saw Him walking on the lake, they were terrified. "It's a ghost," they said, and cried out in fear. But Jesus immediately said to them: "Take courage! It is I. Don't be afraid." "Lord, if it's You," Peter replied, "tell me to come to You on the water." "Come," He said. Then Peter got out of the boat, walked on the water and came toward Jesus. But when he saw the wind, he was afraid and, beginning to sink, cried out, "Lord, save me!"*
> — MATTHEW 14:26-30

Although Peter demonstrated enough confidence and competence to start his miraculous walk on the water (he is still the only person except Jesus who has this feat on his resume), he became unsure of himself when the conditions around him seemed too hostile.

JESUS USING A SUPPORTING STYLE OF LEADERSHIP (S3)
—*High Supportive, Low Directive Behavior*

Capable but cautious performers (D3) need a supporting leadership style (S3)—high supportive, low directive behavior.

Jesus used an appropriate supporting style (S3) when Peter lost confidence. He saved Peter and then reassured him.

> *Immediately Jesus reached out his hand and caught him. "You of little faith," he said, "why did you doubt?"* — MATTHEW 14:31

PETER AS A PEAK PERFORMER (D4)
—*High Competence, High Commitment*

> *"Therefore I let all Israel be assured of this: God has made this Jesus, whom you*
> *crucified, both Lord and Christ." When the people heard this, they were cut to*
> *the heart and said to Peter and the other apostles, "Brothers, what shall we do?"*
> *Peter replied, "Repent and be baptized, every one of you, in the name of Jesus Christ*
> *for the forgiveness of your sins. And you will receive the gift of the Holy Spirit."*
> —ACTS 2:36-38

The same Peter who denied he even knew Jesus now proclaims His
name with the power and confidence of a peak performer.
Although the term Self-Reliant Achiever is also used to describe
this fourth level of development. Peter would probably not claim it
as his own. As he said in 2 Peter 1:3-4:

"His Divine power has given us everything we need for life and goodness
through our knowledge of Him that called us by His own glory and godliness"

JESUS USING A DELEGATING STYLE OF LEADERSHIP (S4)

—Low Supportive, Low Directive Behavior

Peak performers (D4) need a delegating leadership style (S4)—low supportive, low directive behavior.

> Jesus used an appropriate delegating leadership style when the disciples needed to go off on their own to spread the "good news."

> *Jesus came and told His disciples, "I have been given complete authority in heaven and on earth. Therefore, go and make disciples of all the nations, baptizing them in the name of the Father and the Son and the Holy Spirit. Teach these new disciples to obey all the commands I have given you. And be sure of this: I am with you always, even to the end of the age."* — MATTHEW 28:18-20 (NLT)

Did you notice? Jesus did not leave the disciples alone. He said, "I am with you always." This is a key point—delegating does not mean NO Directive or Supportive behaviors. Delegation is not abdication.

The Servant Leader as a Performance Coach.

A key activity of an effective servant leader is to act as a performance coach. When Jesus called them to follow Him, He pledged to the disciples His full support and guidance as they developed into "fishers of men." This is the duty of a servant leader—the ongoing investment of the leader's life into the lives of those who follow. By changing His leadership style appropriately as His disciples developed individually and as a group, Jesus empowered His followers to carry on after He was gone. Through His hands (effective leader behavior) He was able to transmit what was in His heart and head about servant leadership.

Be STILL

and KNOW that

I AM

GOD.

— PSALM 46:10

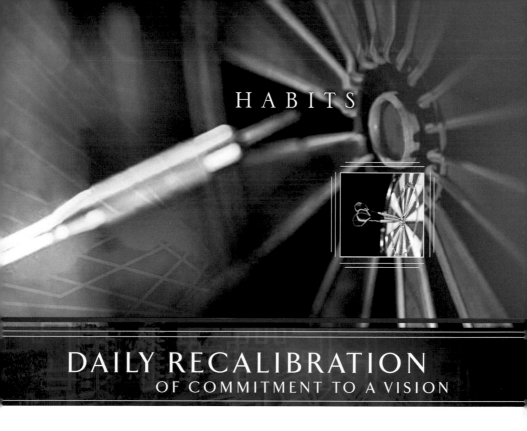

HABITS

DAILY RECALIBRATION
OF COMMITMENT TO A VISION

Before something can become a habit it must first be practiced as a discipline.

The daily pressures of leadership can isolate and diminish a leader's effectiveness and focus. The purpose of the Habits section of this book is to provide an overview of some of the key habits that Jesus modeled for keeping focused and on track with His vision.

On a daily basis, effective servant leaders recalibrate their commitment to their vision—purpose, picture of the future, and values—through the use of five disciplines that were an integral part of what Jesus practiced during His earthly walk:

SOLITUDE — *Spending time alone with God*

PRAYER — *Speaking with God*

STORING UP GOD'S WORD — *Preparing for the challenges that were yet to come*

FAITH IN GOD'S UNCONDITIONAL LOVE — *Proceeding with confidence grounded in trust*

INVOLVEMENT IN ACCOUNTABILITY RELATIONSHIPS — *Sharing His vulnerability*

HABIT #1: SOLITUDE — *Spending time alone with God*

A Call to Solitude. Jesus modeled for us the spiritual discipline of solitude as an essential habit for spiritual renewal. We can be very sure that what He found useful for the conduct of His life in the Father will also be useful for us.

Here are some examples when Jesus engaged in external solitude as a means of fortifying His inner solitude of peace and purpose:

When preparing for the tests of leadership and public ministry, He spent forty days alone in the desert. (Matthew 4:1–11)

Before He chose the Twelve, He spent the entire night alone in the desert hills. (Luke 6:12)

When He had to choose between continuing to heal the sick or move to another place to teach the Good News. *Very early in the morning, while it was still dark, Jesus got up, left the house and went off to a solitary place, where he prayed* (Mark 1:35).

When He received the news of John the Baptist's death, He withdrew from there in a boat to a lonely place apart. (Matthew 14:13)

After the miraculous feeding of the five thousand, Jesus *"went up on a mountainside by himself . . . "* (Matthew 14:23)

By "solitude" we mean being out of human contact, being alone, and being so for lengthy periods of time. To get out of human contact is not something that can be done for a short while, for the contact lingers long after it is, in one sense, over.

Silence is a natural part of solitude and is its essential complement. Most noise is human contact. Silence means to escape from sounds and noises, other than the gentle ones of nature. But it also means not talking, and the effects of not talking on our soul are different from those of simple quietness. Both dimensions of silence are crucial for the breaking of old habits and the formation of Christ's character in us.

Solitude and silence give us some space to reform our innermost attitudes toward people and events. They take the world off our shoulders for a time and interrupt our habit of constantly managing things, of being in control or thinking we are.

One of the greatest of spiritual attainments is the capacity to do nothing. Thus, the Christian philosopher Blaise Pascal insightfully remarks, "I have discovered that all the unhappiness of men arises from one single fact, that they are unable to stay quietly in their room."

"The cure for too much to do is solitude and silence, for there you find that you are safely more than what you do. And a cure of loneliness is solitude and silence, for there you discover in how many ways you are never alone."

How to Engage in Solitude. Find someplace where
you can be totally out of contact with all kinds of human noise (TV,
cell phone, fax, voicemail, that secret pile of paperwork, magazines,
even this book) for a minimum of thirty minutes.

If sitting still is likely to put you to sleep, take a walk. But don't talk
to anyone.

If you are seated in a comfortable position, place your hands on your
knees in a down position. If walking, visualize yourself in this position.
In harmony with the position of your hands, mentally put down everything you are concerned about or expending energy in trying to manage
or control at the foot of the cross. Be specific—name each burden as
you put it down.

When you have exhausted your list, take a couple of deep breaths and
turn your hands, physically and mentally, into an up position and quietly
receive what God reveals to you.

Have no expectations or agenda for this time with God. Let it be
His to fill.

DO NOT BE ANXIOUS ABOUT ANYTHING,
BUT IN EVERYTHING, BY PRAYER AND PETITION,
WITH THANKSGIVING, PRESENT YOUR REQUESTS TO GOD.
AND THE PEACE OF GOD, WHICH TRANSCENDS
ALL UNDERSTANDING, WILL GUARD YOUR HEARTS
AND YOUR MINDS IN CHRIST JESUS.

—PHILIPPIANS 4:6-7

HABIT #2: PRAYER — *Talking with God*

Just suppose prayer was your first response instead of your last resort when facing a new challenge or an old temptation.

The Power and Privilege of Prayer. Prayer is conversing, communicating with God. When we pray we talk to God, aloud or within our thoughts. Prayer almost always involves other disciplines and spiritual activities if it is to go well, especially study, meditation and worship, and often solitude and fasting as well.

It would be a rather low-voltage spiritual life in which prayer was chiefly undertaken as a discipline, rather than as a way of co-laboring with God to accomplish good things and advance His Kingdom purposes. Yet, prayer can be a discipline, and a highly effective one, as we see from our Lord's advice to those with Him in the Garden of Gethsemane: *"Watch and pray so that you will not fall into temptation"* (Matthew 26:41).

Even when we are praying for or about things other than our own spiritual needs and growth, conversing with God cannot fail to have a pervasive and spiritually strengthening effect on all aspects of our personality. That conversation, when it is truly a conversation, makes an indelible impression on our minds, and our consciousness of Him remains vivid as we go our way.

NOW THIS IS THE CONFIDENCE THAT WE HAVE IN HIM,
THAT IF WE ASK ANYTHING ACCORDING TO HIS WILL,
HE HEARS US. AND IF WE KNOW THAT HE HEARS US,
WHATEVER WE ASK, WE KNOW THAT WE HAVE THE PETITIONS
THAT WE HAVE ASKED OF HIM.

—1 JOHN 5:14—15 (NKJV)

How to Pray. A simple acrostic—ACTS—can help you remember the four basic parts of prayer.

ADORATION — This is where all prayers should begin, telling the Lord that you love Him and appreciate all He has done and created.

> *"Praise the LORD, O my soul; all my inmost being, praise his holy name. Praise the LORD, O my soul, and forget not all his benefits"* (Psalm 103:1-2).

CONFESSION — Since we still fall short of God's perfection, we need to make sure that we are cleansed of every sin we have committed.

> *"If we confess our sins, He is faithful and just and will forgive us our sins and purify us from all unrighteousness"* (1 John 1:9).

THANKSGIVING — One of the reasons why Thanksgiving Day is such a treasured holiday is that we truly enjoy being thankful. So why not do it every day? During this part of your prayer, thank God specifically for all that He did for you since the last time you talked.

> *"Sing and make music in your heart to the Lord, always giving thanks to God the Father for everything, in the name of our Lord Jesus Christ"* (Ephesians 5:19-20).

SUPPLICATION — This is just a big word for asking for what you need. Start with prayers for others and then ask for your own needs to be met. It's okay to have a big "wish list." According to God's Word, we can ask with confidence.

> *"Ask and it will be given to you; seek and you will find; knock and the door will be opened to you"* (Matthew 7:7).

HABIT #3: STORING UP THE WORD OF GOD
— Preparing for the challenges that lie ahead

The discipline of memorizing Scripture will pay off big dividends when you meet a challenge or temptation you don't know how to handle.

DO NOT CONFORM ANY LONGER TO THE PATTERN OF THIS WORLD.
BUT BE TRANSFORMED BY THE RENEWING OF YOUR MIND.
THEN YOU WILL BE ABLE TO TEST AND APPROVE WHAT GOD'S WILL IS
—HIS GOOD, PLEASING, AND PERFECT WILL.

— ROMANS 12:2

ALL SCRIPTURE IS GOD—BREATHED AND IS USEFUL FOR TEACHING,
REBUKING, CORRECTING, AND TRAINING IN RIGHTEOUSNESS,
SO THAT THE MAN OF GOD MAY BE THOROUGHLY EQUIPPED FOR
EVERY GOOD WORK.

— 2 TIMOTHY 3:16-17

IF YOU REMAIN IN ME AND MY WORDS REMAIN IN YOU,
ASK WHATEVER YOU WISH, AND IT WILL BE GIVEN TO YOU.

— JOHN 15:7

4560.90
Chem. com
LUKE. 19
LUKE. 20.
Jesus enters Jerusalem

A Wake-up Call.

A wise person once said, "Life is like a tube of toothpaste; you never know what's inside until you're squeezed." In times of personal crisis, you have to call on the resources of faith that you've already stored up.

·A LITTLE SLEEP, A LITTLE SLUMBER,
A LITTLE FOLDING OF THE HANDS TO REST
AND POVERTY WILL COME ON YOU LIKE A BANDIT
AND SCARCITY LIKE AN ARMED MAN.

— PROVERBS 6:10—22

Maybe it's time for you to crawl out from under the covers of complacency and replenish your spiritual resources or risk being caught unprepared when the next challenge or temptation comes your way.

FOR GOD SO LOVED THE WORLD THAT HE GAVE
HIS ONE AND ONLY SON, THAT WHOEVER BELIEVES IN HIM
SHALL NOT PERISH BUT HAVE ETERNAL LIFE.

— JOHN 3:16

HABIT #4: FAITH IN UNCONDITIONAL LOVE

— Proceeding with confidence grounded in trust

Jesus set the standard for us on unconditional love.
It was just before the Passover Feast. Jesus knew that the time
had come for Him to leave this world and go to the Father. Having
loved His own who were in the world, He now showed them the
full extent of His love. *(John 13:1)*

What does unconditional love mean for the servant leader?

1. Accepting that you are unconditionally loved.
   "For God so loved YOU . . ."

2. You must unconditionally love the people around you.
   *"A new command I give you: Love one another. As I have loved you,
   so you must love one another"* (John 13:34).

   Love those at home. Love those at work.
   Love the cafeteria server. Love the potential client.
   Love whomever you encounter.

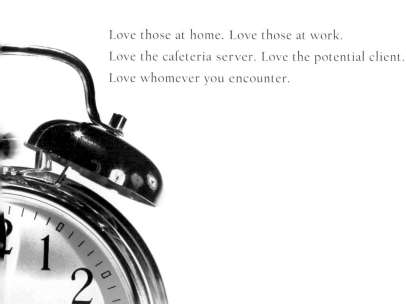

So much of what we're talking about in servant leadership has to do with the human ego and your capacity to accept the unconditional love that is there for you.

For example, suppose we asked parents, "How many of you love your kids?" Undoubtedly all would say they do. Then if we asked them, "How many of you love your kids only if they're successful? If they're successful you love them; if they're not, you don't." Few, if any, would answer in the affirmative. Why? Because as parents, you love your kids unconditionally, right?

What if you accepted that unconditional love for yourself? What if you realized that you can't win enough, accomplish enough, write enough, control enough, have enough to get any more love—you've already got all the love there is. That would be so powerful! Once you accept that you're unconditionally loved, then earthly things don't mislead you.

God clearly showed His unconditional love for us when He gave Jesus to die in our place.

The antidote for fear and pride is faith in God's unconditional love for us. The true servant leader is one who clearly understands what unconditional love is all about and puts it into practice every day.

Servant leaders understand that everyone needs to be heard, praised, encouraged, forgiven, accepted and guided back to the right path when they drift off course. As leaders, we need to practice these behaviors. Why? Because Jesus did!

Two are better than one, because they
have a good return for their work:
if one falls down, his friend can help him up.
But pity the man who falls
and has no one to help him up. . . .
Though one may be overpowered
two can defend themselves.
A cord of three strands is not quickly broken.

—Ecclesiastes 4:9–10, 12

As iron sharpens iron,
so one man sharpens another."

—Proverbs 27:17

HABIT #5: ACCOUNTABILITY RELATIONSHIPS
— *Sharing vulnerability, receiving support and being held accountable*

Leadership is a very lonely business. When we rely on our own perspective of how we are doing, we are bound to slip into convenient rationalizations and blind spots that can quickly invalidate the integrity of our witness to a watching world.

THE ANTIDOTE FOR FEAR AND PRIDE
IS TRUST IN GOD'S UNCONDITIONAL LOVE FOR US.

Encouragement and Feedback.

We do the best we can—we plan, we strategize, we act—but still we all need some outside information to help us see how we're doing.

THE CRUCIBLE FOR SILVER
AND THE FURNACE FOR GOLD.
BUT A MAN IS TESTED
BY THE PRAISE HE RECEIVES.

—PROVERBS 27:21

WOUNDS FROM A FRIEND CAN BE TRUSTED.
BUT AN ENEMY MULTIPLIES KISSES.

—PROVERBS 27:6

Truth-Tellers. We all need trusted truth-tellers, preferably those not directly impacted by what we do, who can help us keep on course. If you can't name any active truth-tellers in your life or if you have avoided or undervalued the ones you have, it's time for a change.

Having truth-tellers in your life is important. It's probably your greatest opportunity for growth. There are two main ways that growth takes place:

> » *When you're open to feedback from other people*
>
> » *When you're willing to disclose your vulnerabilities to other people*

So it's a two-way process.

Disclosing your vulnerabilities doesn't mean expressing all your inner thoughts. Rather, you want to share task-relevant information, struggles you're working on as a leader.

If a truth-teller says that you're not a good listener, then what a wonderful thing to come in front of that team and share that. "So-and-so was kind enough to share feedback with me about my listening. I didn't realize that when you would say things to me, I would jump right on to my own agenda. But now I know and I would like to improve it, and the only way I can improve it is if you will help me."

Too often in organizations, self-serving leaders cut off feedback by killing the messenger. Eventually the anti-feedback leader gets blindsided even though people were available who could have given helpful information.

Feedback is a gift. If somebody gives you a gift, what do you say to them? "Thank you." Then you say: "Where did you get it? Are there any special instructions to help me use it? Can you tell me more about it? Who else do I need to ask about it?"

We're all vulnerable. We all fall short. Don't be afraid to share your vulnerability. It's one of the most powerful things you can do to build a team, to build a relationship with people you're leading. They know you're not perfect, so don't act it.

Bring truth-tellers into your life, and they'll be there if they know that you'll listen. It doesn't mean you have to do everything that they say, but they want to be heard. And in the process if you'll share some of your vulnerability, then that give and take is fabulous.

As an interesting Bible study on the value of having a truth teller, read Exodus 18:13-27. See how Moses, one of the greatest leaders of all time, and those who looked to him for leadership benefited from a trusted truth-teller.

In Exodus 18:13–27 (NKJV) we read:

> [13]And so it was, on the next day, that Moses sat to judge the people; and the people stood before Moses from morning until evening. [14]So when Moses' father-in-law saw all that he did for the people, he said, "What is this thing that you are doing for the people? Why do you alone sit, and all the people stand before you from morning until evening?" [15]And Moses said to his father-in-law, "Because the people come to me to inquire of God. [16]When they have a difficulty, they come to me, and I judge between one and another; and I make known the statutes of God and His laws."

Moses knew Jethro was a truth-teller, so he listened when his father-in-law offered suggestions for how the people of Israel should be governed.

> [17]So Moses' father-in-law said to him, "The thing that you do is not good. [18]Both you and these people who are with you will surely wear yourselves out. For this thing is too much for you; you are not able to perform it by yourself. [19]Listen now to my voice; I will give you counsel and God will be with you: Stand before God for the people, so that you may bring the difficulties to God. [20]And you shall teach them the statutes and the laws, and show them the way in which they must walk and the work they must do. [21]Moreover you shall select from all the people able men, such as fear God, men of truth, hating covetousness; and place such over them to be rulers of thousands, rulers of hundreds, rulers of fifties, and rulers of tens. [22]And let them judge the people at all times. Then it will be that every great matter they shall bring to you, but every small matter they themselves shall judge. So it will be easier for you, for they will bear the burden with you. [23]If you do this thing,

and God so commands you, then you will be able to endure, and all this people will also go to their place in peace." ²⁴So Moses heeded the voice of his father-in-law and did all that he had said. ²⁵And Moses chose able men out of all Israel, and made them heads over the people: rulers of thousands, rulers of hundreds, rulers of fifties, and rulers of tens. ²⁶So they judged the people at all times; the hard cases they brought to Moses, but they judged every small case themselves.

²⁷Then Moses let his father-in-law depart, and he went his way to his own land.

Even great leaders like Moses can fall victim to their own blind spots. When they do, their effectiveness and credibility as a leader can be impacted unless they have people in their life who have been given permission to call them to task when they get off track.

Accountability Fellowship.

In *Leadership by the Book*, Michael, one of the central characters, explains how he got into trouble after a successful start at becoming a servant leader. Michael explained, "When I boil it down, it was a combination of ego and self-imposed isolation."

Throughout His earthly ministry, Jesus maintained a special, intimate relationship with a small group of His disciples.

To put things in perspective, Jesus had:

> » *Hundreds, or even thousands, of people flocking*
> *to Him everywhere He went*

> » *Dozens of men and women who followed Him*
> *consistently from town to town*

> » *Twelve specially chosen disciples to whom*
> *He entrusted His mission*

> » *Three inner-circle friends to lean on in crucial times*

In Mark 9:2–12 we are told that Jesus took Peter, James, and John with Him to a high mountain and revealed to them the full reality of His God nature. There He instructed them to keep what they had observed in confidence.

In Mark 14:33 Jesus again gathered the same three men to Himself as He approached the trials He was about to undertake. In doing so, Jesus demonstrated how much He valued the fellowship of those who knew Him best while He was going through a rough time.

As we commit to becoming more like Jesus in our leadership service, it is vital that we don't miss the important example Christ provided on how to combat the loneliness and isolation that can often be a part of being a leader.

Each of us can benefit from similar relationships if we are to maintain and grow in our daily walk as Jesus-like leaders. The temptations and challenges of ego-driven and fear-motivated leadership are going to continue and probably intensify. The value of having a safe harbor relationship of support and accountability cannot be overemphasized.

LET US CONSIDER HOW WE MAY
SPUR ONE ANOTHER ON
TOWARD LOVE AND GOOD DEEDS.
LET US NOT GIVE UP MEETING TOGETHER . . .
BUT LET US ENCOURAGE ONE ANOTHER.

—HEBREWS 10:24–25

SHEPHERD THE FLOCK OF GOD . . .
WHICH IS AMONG YOU, SERVING AS OVERSEERS,
NOT BY COMPULSION BUT WILLINGLY,
NOT FOR DISHONEST GAIN BUT EAGERLY;
NOR AS BEING LORDS OVER THOSE
ENTRUSTED TO YOU,
BUT BEING EXAMPLES TO THE FLOCK;
AND WHEN THE CHIEF SHEPHERD APPEARS,
YOU WILL RECEIVE THE CROWN OF GLORY
THAT DOES NOT FADE AWAY.

—1 PETER 5:2–4 (NKJV)

CONCLUSION

NEXT STEPS AND
RESOURCES

Living Servant Leadership. We hope this book is
the beginning of a life-changing experience.

The real challenge starts now as you encounter the world that is waiting
for you. Your email is downloading. Your voicemail is full. People have
demands on you. Your family wants you to do this and that. So you're
going to need a very, very clear plan in order to maintain and use the
servant leadership concepts you've learned. That's important. That's the
mandate from Jesus. It's not voluntary.

Let us suggest some next steps to get you started in bringing these
ideas into your real world.

>> *First, flip through this book again periodically to review key points—especially things that you think you need to do to change your behavior as a leader.*

>> *The second thing is to share what you've learned with people who look to you for leadership at work, at church or at home. Ask them to be your truth-tellers. Leadership is not something you do to people; it's something you do with people.*

>> *The third thing is you want to think through how you enter your day, because the habits that Jesus used to keep Himself focused are important to you, too. They can be implemented well if you plan how you enter your day. You need solitude, you need prayer time, and you need time to study the Scriptures. So work on your habits. Make sure they are organized to help you stay true to your desire to be a servant leader.*

Jesus is the master of the art of living and leading as an act of service. He loves it when you call on Him. He is only a prayer away as your leadership guide and inspiration. You're not called to lead by yourself.

> *3Jesus, knowing that the Father had given all things into His hands, and that He had come from God and was going to God, 4rose from supper and laid aside His garments, took a towel and girded Himself. 5After that, He poured water into a basin and began to wash the disciples' feet, and to wipe them with the towel with which He was girded.*

> *12So when He had washed their feet, taken His garments, and sat down again, He said to them, "Do you know what I have done to you? 13You call Me Teacher and Lord, and you say well, for so I am. 14If I then, your Lord and Teacher, have washed your feet, you also ought to wash one another's feet. 15For I have given you an example, that you should do as I have done to you. 16Most assuredly, I say to you, a servant is not greater than his master; nor is he who is sent greater than he who sent him. 17If you know these things, blessed are you if you do them."* —JOHN 13:3-5 & 13:12-17 (NKJV)

CHECKLIST OF ESSENTIALS
FOR SERVANT LEADERS

Below is a checklist of tools every servant leader needs.

[ ] *Personal mission statement that is easy to understand and remember.*

[ ] *Personal definition of success that keeps God in mind.*

[ ] *Set of rank-ordered personal operating values to help you decide which road to travel when temptation or opportunity knocks.*

[ ] *Two or three truth-tellers who will keep you headed in the right direction.*

[ ] *Journal to record the triumphs, challenges, and lessons learned that you will want to remember and pass along to others.*

[ ] *Well-used instruction manual for daily living.*

[ ] *Set of positive addictions to solitude, prayer, and study of scripture, rest and exercise.*

[ ] *A memorized set of "emergency numbers" to call when you are in trouble.*

Emergency Numbers

FEAR

Be anxious for nothing, but in everything
by prayer and supplication, with thanksgiving,
let your requests be made known to God;
and the peace of God, which surpasses
all understanding, will guard your hearts
and minds through Christ Jesus.
— Philippians 4:6–7

The LORD is my shepherd; I shall not want.
He makes me to lie down in green pastures;
He leads me beside the still waters.
He restores my soul; He leads me in the paths
of righteousness For His name's sake.
Yea, though I walk through the valley
of the shadow of death,
I will fear no evil; For You are with me;
Your rod and Your staff, they comfort me.
You prepare a table before me
in the presence of my enemies;
You anoint my head with oil; My cup runs over.
Surely goodness and mercy shall follow me
All the days of my life; And I will dwell
in the house of the LORD Forever.
— Psalm 23

ANXIETY

CAST YOUR BURDEN ON THE LORD,
AND HE SHALL SUSTAIN YOU;
HE SHALL NEVER PERMIT
THE RIGHTEOUS TO BE MOVED.
—PSALM 55:22

WORRY

THEREFORE I SAY TO YOU, DO NOT WORRY ABOUT YOUR LIFE,
WHAT YOU WILL EAT OR WHAT YOU WILL DRINK;
NOR ABOUT YOUR BODY, WHAT YOU WILL PUT ON. IS NOT LIFE
MORE THAN FOOD AND THE BODY MORE THAN CLOTHING?
—MATTHEW 6:25

TEMPTATION

NO TEMPTATION HAS OVERTAKEN YOU EXCEPT
SUCH AS IS COMMON TO MAN; BUT GOD IS FAITHFUL,
WHO WILL NOT ALLOW YOU TO BE TEMPTED
BEYOND WHAT YOU ARE ABLE, BUT WITH THE TEMPTATION
WILL ALSO MAKE THE WAY OF ESCAPE,
THAT YOU MAY BE ABLE TO BEAR IT
—1 CORINTHIANS 10:13.

PRIDE

FOR I SAY, THROUGH THE GRACE GIVEN TO ME,
TO EVERYONE WHO IS AMONG YOU,
NOT TO THINK OF HIMSELF MORE HIGHLY
THAN HE OUGHT TO THINK, BUT TO THINK SOBERLY,
AS GOD HAS DEALT TO EACH ONE A MEASURE OF FAITH.
— ROMANS 12:3

BY PRIDE COMES NOTHING BUT STRIFE,
BUT WITH THE WELL—ADVISED IS WISDOM.
— PROVERBS 13:10

VALUES

THUS SAYS THE LORD:
"LET NOT THE WISE MAN GLORY IN HIS WISDOM,
LET NOT THE MIGHTY MAN GLORY IN HIS MIGHT,
NOR LET THE RICH MAN GLORY IN HIS RICHES;
BUT LET HIM WHO GLORIES GLORY IN THIS,
THAT HE UNDERSTANDS AND KNOWS ME,
THAT I AM THE LORD, EXERCISING LOVINGKINDNESS,
JUDGMENT, AND RIGHTEOUSNESS IN THE EARTH.
FOR IN THESE I DELIGHT," SAYS THE LORD.
— JEREMIAH 9:23—24

REPENTANCE

IF WE CONFESS OUR SINS,
HE IS FAITHFUL AND JUST TO FORGIVE
US OUR SINS AND TO CLEANSE US
FROM ALL UNRIGHTEOUSNESS.
— 1 JOHN 1:9

GUIDANCE

TRUST IN THE LORD WITH ALL YOUR HEART,
AND LEAN NOT ON YOUR OWN UNDERSTANDING;
IN ALL YOUR WAYS ACKNOWLEDGE HIM,
AND HE SHALL DIRECT YOUR PATHS.
— PROVERBS 3:5-6

TEACH ME TO DO YOUR WILL,
FOR YOU ARE MY GOD;
YOUR SPIRIT IS GOOD.
LEAD ME IN THE LAND OF UPRIGHTNESS.
— PSALM 143:10

If I then, your LORD and Teacher,

have washed your feet,

YOU also ought to

wash one another's feet.

For I have given you an EXAMPLE,

that YOU SHOULD DO

as I HAVE DONE TO YOU.

— JOHN 13:14-15

My Commitment
to Servant Leadership

You've read the book, now it's time for you to take the next steps into your journey as a servant leader.

I, _____, commit to God, myself, and one other person to accomplishing the following next steps in becoming a more Jesus-like servant leader during the next thirty days.

In seeking a closer discipleship relationship with Jesus as my leadership role model through practicing the spiritual disciplines of solitude, prayer, study of God's Word, unconditional love, and support and accountability relationships, I will:

_____

_____

_____

In each of the following relationships in which I serve a leadership role, I will demonstrate my commitment to Jesus-like leadership.

With those who report to me I will:

_____

_____

With my peers I will:

_____

_____

With those to whom I report I will:

_____

_____

With my family and friends I will:

_____

_____

In being held accountable for my ongoing steps to becoming a more
Jesus-like leader, I will seek the support of the following people:

_____

_____

_____

In the next thirty days I will teach what I have learned about being
a Jesus-like servant leader to the following people who are important
to me:

_____

_____

_____

Signed _____

Date _____

SERVANT LEADERSHIP

STARTS WITH A VISION

AND ENDS WITH A SERVANT HEART

THAT HELPS PEOPLE

LIVE ACCORDING TO THAT VISION.

ACKNOWLEDGEMENTS

This book would not have come together
without the efforts and support of the following people:
Our wives, **Margie Blanchard** and **Jane Hodges**,
The wonderful editorial work of **Kathy Baker**,
Our administrative and support team,
Dottie Hamilt, Anna Espino, and **Marsha Wilson**
Our colleagues at the Center for *FaithWalk* Leadership,
Lee Ross, Phyllis Hendry, and **Vince Siciliano**

We are indebted to the wisdom and writings of the following authors:

The One–Minute Manager®
KEN BLANCHARD & SPENCER JOHNSON

The Search for Significance
ROBERT MCGEE

Celebration of Discipline
RICHARD J. FOSTER

The Divine Conspiracy
DALLAS WILLARD

Half Time
BOB BUFORD

Leadership by the Book
KEN BLANCHARD, PHIL HODGES, BILL HYBELS

Servanthood
BENNET J. SIMS

And most of all, we owe thanks to our three chief Consultants:
The Father, The Son, and **The Holy Spirit**

About the Authors

Dr. Ken Blanchard is the Chief Spiritual Officer of The Ken Blanchard Companies, a full-service management consulting and training company that he and his wife, Dr. Marjorie Blanchard, founded in 1979. Ken co-authored the best-selling book *The One-Minute Manager*® with Spencer Johnson, and the book has sold more than ten million copies and has been translated into more than twenty-five languages. Some of his recent books are: *Raving Fans* (with Sheldon Bowles), *Gung Ho* (with Sheldon Bowles), *Leadership by the Book* (with Phil Hodges and Bill Hybels), *Whale Done* (with Thad Lacinak, Chuck Thompkins, and Jim Ballard), *The Generosity Factor* (with S. Truett Cathy), and *The One-Minute Apology* (with Margret McBride). Ken is one of today's most sought-after authors, speakers and business consultants, and he is cofounder of the Center for *FaithWalk* Leadership.

Phil Hodges is cofounder and vice chairman of the Center for *FaithWalk* Leadership. The mission of the Center is to challenge and equip people to *Lead Like Jesus*. After thirty-five years as a human resources and industrial relations professional with Xerox Corporation and U.S. Steel, Phil joined the Ken Blanchard Companies in 1998 as a management consultant and trainer in leadership and customer service programs. In addition to helping leaders of faith walk their talk in the marketplace, Phil has developed a passion for bringing the *Lead Like Jesus* message into the church. Phil and his wife, Jane, live in Rancho Palos Verdes, California.

FOR MORE INFORMATION

The Center for *FaithWalk* Leadership
is a non-profit organization that advocates,
challenges, and equips people to
Lead Like Jesus.

For more information on the Center for
FaithWalk Leadership and its
Lead Like Jesus seminars
and resources, contact:

www.faithwalkleadership.com

1229 Augusta West Parkway
Augusta, GA 30909
VOICE (706) 863-8494
FAX (706) 863-9372